Love Letters

First Edition
26 25 24 23 22   5 4 3 2 1

Published by
Gibbs Smith
P.O. Box 667
Layton, Utah 84041

1.800.835.4993 orders
www.gibbs-smith.com

Printed and bound in China

Gibbs Smith books are printed on either recycled, 100% post-
consumer waste, FSC-certified papers or on paper produced from
sustainable PEFC-certified forest/controlled wood source. Learn
more at www.pefc.org.
Library of Congress Control Number: 2022930941

ISBN: 978-1-4236-6156-6

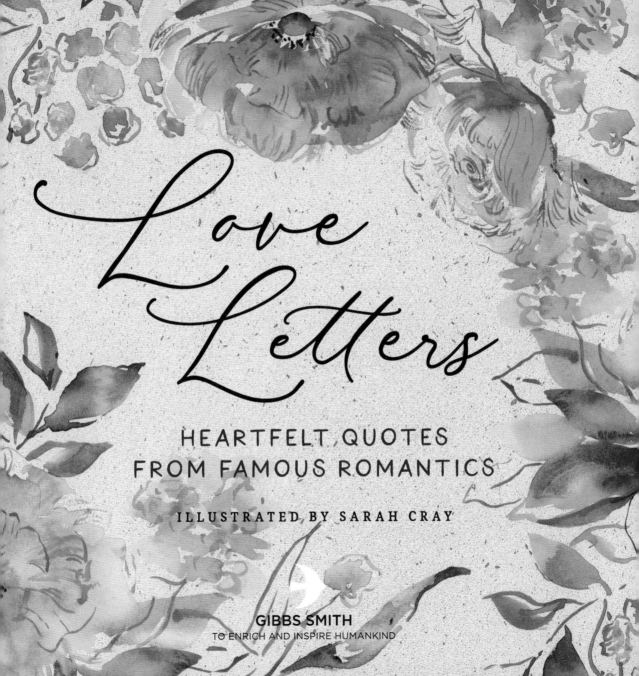

Love Letters

HEARTFELT QUOTES
FROM FAMOUS ROMANTICS

ILLUSTRATED BY SARAH CRAY

GIBBS SMITH
TO ENRICH AND INSPIRE HUMANKIND

Should I draw you the picture of my heart, it would be what I hope you would still love though it contained nothing new.

The early possession you obtained there, and the absolute power you have obtained over it, leaves not the smallest space unoccupied.

ABIGAIL ADAMS TO JOHN ADAMS

O HEART O LOVE EVERYTHING

IS SUDDENLY TURNED TO GOLD!

DON'T BE AFRAID

DON'T WORRY

THE MOST ASTOUNDING BEAUTIFUL

THING HAS HAPPENED HERE!

Allen Ginsberg to Peter Orlovsky

*Your word travels the
entirety of space and reaches
my cells which are my
stars then goes to yours
which are my light.*

FRIDA KAHLO TO DIEGO RIVERA

You are not only the solar spectrum with the seven luminous colors, but the sun himself, that illumines, warms, and revivifies!

JULIETTE DROUET TO VICTOR HUGO

I love you more than anybody in the world. . . . I love you for millions and millions of things, clocks and vampires and dirty nails and squiggly paintings and lovely hair and being dizzy and falling dreams.

DYLAN THOMAS TO CAITLIN THOMAS

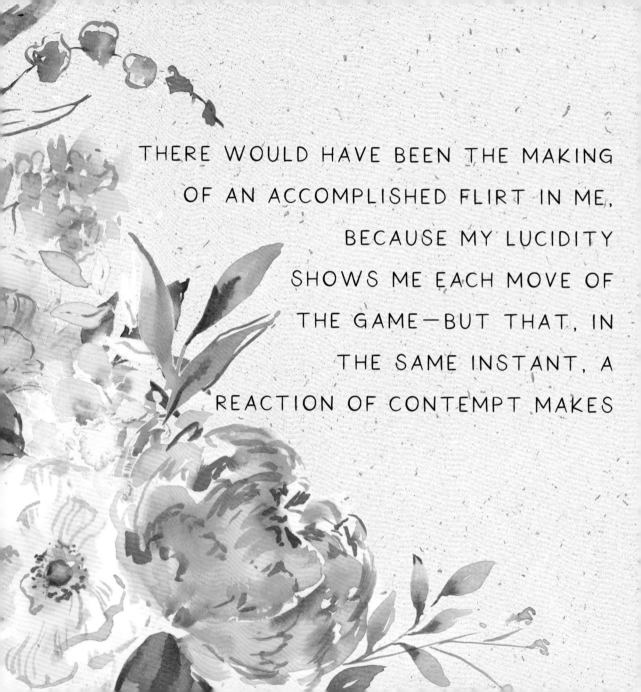

THERE WOULD HAVE BEEN THE MAKING OF AN ACCOMPLISHED FLIRT IN ME, BECAUSE MY LUCIDITY SHOWS ME EACH MOVE OF THE GAME—BUT THAT, IN THE SAME INSTANT, A REACTION OF CONTEMPT MAKES

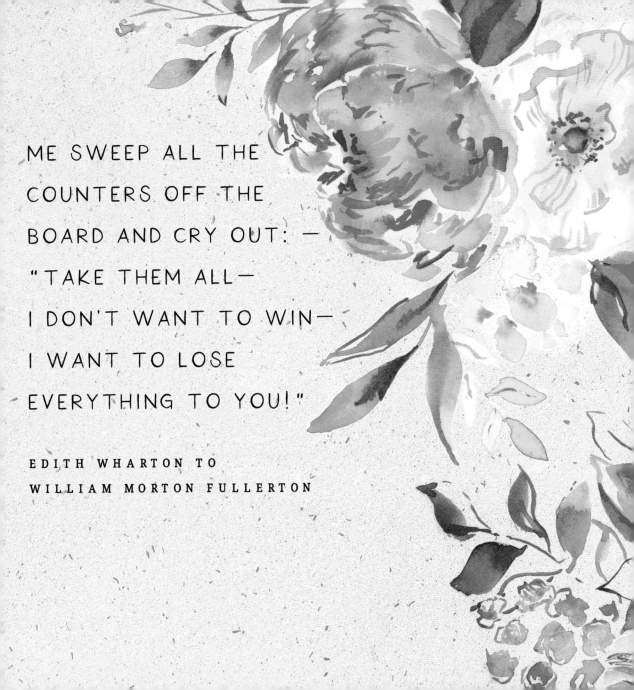

ME SWEEP ALL THE
COUNTERS OFF THE
BOARD AND CRY OUT: —
"TAKE THEM ALL—
I DON'T WANT TO WIN—
I WANT TO LOSE
EVERYTHING TO YOU!"

EDITH WHARTON TO
WILLIAM MORTON FULLERTON

I couldn't say je t'aime and je t'adore as I longed to do, but always remember that I am saying it, that I go to sleep thinking of you.

ELEANOR ROOSEVELT TO LORENA HICKOK

YOU HAVE TOUCHED ME MORE
PROFOUNDLY THAN I THOUGHT EVEN
YOU COULD HAVE TOUCHED ME—
MY HEART WAS FULL WHEN YOU
CAME HERE TODAY.
HENCEFORWARD I AM YOURS
FOR EVERYTHING.

*Elizabeth Barrett Browning to
Robert Browning*

I can't say how every time
I ever put my arms around you
I felt that I was home.

ERNEST HEMINGWAY TO MARLENE DIETRICH

I love her, and that's the beginning and end of everything.

F. SCOTT FITZGERALD TO
ZELDA FITZGERALD

IF ONLY I WERE A CLEVER
WOMAN, I COULD DESCRIBE
TO YOU MY GORGEOUS
BIRD, HOW YOU UNITE IN
YOURSELF THE BEAUTIES OF
FORM, PLUMAGE, AND SONG!
I WOULD TELL YOU THAT
YOU ARE THE GREATEST
MARVEL OF ALL AGES, AND I
SHOULD ONLY BE SPEAKING
THE SIMPLE TRUTH.

JULIETTE DROUET TO
VICTOR HUGO

I belong to you; there is really no other way of expressing it, and that is not strong enough.

FRANZ KAFKA TO
FELICE BAUER

My body is filled with you for days and days. You are the mirror of the night. The violent flash of lightning. The dampness of the earth.

FRIDA KAHLO TO DIEGO RIVERA

*My whole desire
was to live
in love, absorbing
passionate devotion to
one person.*

HARRIET BEECHER STOWE TO
CALVIN ELLIS STOWE

GIVE ME A FEW DAYS OF PEACE

IN YOUR ARMS—

I NEED IT TERRIBLY.

I'M RAGGED, WORN, EXHAUSTED.

AFTER THAT I CAN FACE

THE WORLD.

Henry Miller to Anaïs Nin

Yesterday, during the whole evening, I said to myself "She is mine!" Ah! The angels are not as happy in Paradise as I was yesterday!

HONORÉ DE BALZAC TO EVELINA HANSKA

If I know what love is,

it is because of you.

HERMANN HESSE,
Narcissus and Goldmund

YOU PIERCE MY SOUL. . . .
I OFFER MYSELF TO YOU
AGAIN WITH A HEART
EVEN MORE YOUR OWN

JANE AUSTEN,
Persuasion

I DON'T KNOW WHAT IS THE MATTER
WITH ME. I AM SO EXULTED. I AM
ALMOST MAD, WORKING, LOVING YOU,
WRITING, AND THINKING OF YOU,
PLAYING YOUR RECORDS, DANCING IN THE
ROOM WHEN MY EYES ARE TIRED. YOU
HAVE GIVEN ME SUCH JOYS THAT IT DOES
NOT MATTER WHAT HAPPENS NOW.

Anaïs Nin to Henry Miller

Tonight I love you

on a spring evening.

I love you with

the window open.

JEAN-PAUL SARTRE TO SIMONE JOLLIVET

I ALMOST WISH WE WERE
BUTTERFLIES AND LIV'D BUT THREE
SUMMER DAYS—THREE SUCH DAYS
WITH YOU I COULD FILL WITH MORE
DELIGHT THAN FIFTY COMMON YEARS
COULD EVER CONTAIN.

John Keats to Fanny Brawne

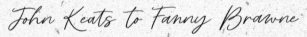

In spite of myself, my imagination carries me to you.

HONORÉ DE BALZAC TO
EVELINA HANSKA

I CANNOT GET THAT BEAUTIFUL
AFTERNOON OUT OF MY HEAD, ABOVE
ME WHERE I LAY, THE GRASS WAS
SILHOUETTED AGAINST THE BLUE OF
THE HEAVENS, SMALL CLOUDS WERE
RUSHING PAST AS THE WIND DROVE
THEM ON AN ENDLESS JOURNEY. THEN
CLOSE TO ME WAS THE MOST LOVELY
OF ALL, YOUR SOFT HAIR AGAINST MY
CHEEK, YOUR KISSES SO COOL AND
UNEARTHLY, AND MY HAPPINESS
WAS SO GREAT.

Julia Lee Booker to Pat McSwiney

You might drop your
heart into me and you'd never
hear it touch bottom.

KATHERINE MANSFIELD TO
JOHN MIDDLETON MURRY

I ALREADY LOVE IN YOU YOUR BEAUTY, BUT I AM ONLY BEGINNING TO LOVE IN YOU THAT WHICH IS ETERNAL AND EVER PRECIOUS— YOUR HEART, YOUR SOUL.

Leo Tolstoy to Valeria Arsenev

*I feel I exist here, and I feel
I shall exist hereafter, —to what
purpose you will decide;
my destiny rests with you.*

LORD BYRON TO COUNTESS TERESA GUICCIOLI

Oh, continue to love me— never misjudge the most faithful heart of your beloved. Ever thine. Ever mine. Ever ours.

LUDWIG VAN BEETHOVEN TO
HIS IMMORTAL BELOVED

I'd like to paint you, but there are
no colors, because there are so many,
in my confusion, the tangible
form of my great love.

FRIDA KAHLO TO DIEGO RIVERA

Out of the depths of
my happy heart wells a great
tide of love and prayer
for this priceless treasure
that is confined to my
life-long keeping.

MARK TWAIN TO OLIVIA LANGDON

WHEN, FREE FROM ALL
SOLICITUDE, ALL
HARASSING CARE,
SHALL I BE ABLE TO PASS
ALL MY TIME WITH YOU,
HAVING ONLY TO LOVE
YOU, AND TO THINK ONLY
OF THE HAPPINESS OF SO
SAYING, AND OF
PROVING IT TO YOU?

Napoléon Bonaparte to
Joséphine de Beauharnais

Life seems emptier without you, the soulwarmth isn't around.

ALLEN GINSBERG TO
PETER ORLOVSKY

DEAREST, I WISH I HAD THE
GIFT OF MAKING RHYMES, FOR
METHINKS THERE IS POETRY
IN MY HEAD AND HEART SINCE I
HAVE BEEN IN LOVE WITH YOU. YOU
ARE A POEM. OF WHAT SORT, THEN? EPIC?
MERCY ON ME, NO! A SONNET? NO;

FOR THAT IS TOO LABORED AND
ARTIFICIAL. YOU ARE A SORT OF
SWEET, SIMPLE, GAY, PATHETIC
BALLAD, WHICH NATURE IS SINGING,
SOMETIMES WITH TEARS, SOMETIMES
WITH SMILES, AND SOMETIMES WITH
INTERMINGLED SMILES AND TEARS.

Nathaniel Hawthorne to
Sophia Hawthorne

TONIGHT I LOVE YOU IN A WAY
THAT YOU HAVE NOT KNOWN IN
ME: I AM NEITHER WORN DOWN
BY TRAVELS NOR WRAPPED UP IN
THE DESIRE FOR YOUR PRESENCE. I
AM MASTERING MY LOVE FOR YOU
AND TURNING IT INWARDS AS A
CONSTITUENT ELEMENT OF MYSELF.

Jean-Paul Sartre to Simone Jollivet

BEAUTIFUL, PRECIOUS LITTLE BABY—
HURRY UP THE SUN!—MAKE THE DAYS
SHORTER TILL WE MEET. I LOVE YOU,
THAT'S ALL THERE IS TO IT.

ORSON WELLES TO RITA HAYWORTH

You cannot see its intangible waves as they flow towards you, darling, but in these lines you will hear, as it were, the distant beating of the surf.

MARK TWAIN TO OLIVIA LANGDON

YOUR SLIM GILT SOUL WALKS
BETWEEN PASSION AND POETRY.
I KNOW HYACINTHUS, WHOM
APOLLO LOVED SO MADLY,
WAS YOU IN GREEK DAYS.

OSCAR WILDE TO
LORD ALFRED DOUGLAS

*Of all your work, you are
still your most beautiful.
The most beautiful work of all.*

PATTI SMITH TO
ROBERT MAPPLETHORPE

EVEN IN MY DREAMS I NEVER
IMAGINED THAT I SHOULD FIND
SO MUCH LOVE ON EARTH. HOW
THAT MOMENT SHINES FOR ME
STILL WHEN I WAS CLOSE TO
YOU, WITH YOUR HAND IN MINE.

Prince Albert to Queen Victoria

I don't want to live—
I want to love first,
and live incidentally.

ZELDA FITZGERALD TO
F. SCOTT FITZGERALD

WITH ALL THE LOVE IN THE
WORLD AND AS ALWAYS, A
MILLION HEARTFELT THANKS FOR
BRINGING SUCH JOY INTO THIS
PARTICULAR CHICK'S LIFE.

Princess Diana to Dodi Fayed

AND WHEN THE WIND BLOWS AND
THE RAINS FALL AND THE SUN SHINES
THROUGH THE CLOUDS (AS IT IS
NOW) HE STILL RESOLVES, AS HE DID
THEN, THAT NOTHING SO FINE EVER
HAPPENED TO HIM OR ANYONE ELSE
AS FALLING IN LOVE WITH THEE—
MY DEAREST HEART.

RICHARD NIXON TO PAT RYAN NIXON

As for my heart, there you will always be—very much so. I have a delicious sense of you there.

HONORÉ DE BALZAC TO
EVELINA HANSKA

I HAVE A THOUSAND IMAGES OF YOU
IN AN HOUR; ALL DIFFERENT AND
ALL COMING BACK TO THE SAME.
I THINK OF YOU ONCE AGAINST A
SKYLINE: AND ON THE HILL THAT
SUNDAY MORNING. THE LIGHT AND
THE SHADOW AND QUIETNESS AND
THE RAIN AND THE WOOD. AND YOU.
YOUR ARMS AND LIPS AND HAIR
AND SHOULDERS AND VOICE — YOU

Rupert Brooke to Noel Olivier

BUT I MORE THAN LOVE YOU,
AND CANNOT CEASE TO LOVE YOU.

Lord Byron to
Countess Teresa Guiccioli

I just miss you, in a quite simple desperate human way.

VITA SACKVILLE-WEST TO
VIRGINIA WOOLF

Come live in my
heart, and pay no rent.

SAMUEL LOVER,
Live in my Heart and Pay No Rent

I LOVE YOU BECAUSE I LOVE YOU,
BECAUSE IT WOULD BE IMPOSSIBLE
FOR ME NOT TO LOVE YOU. I
LOVE YOU WITHOUT QUESTION,
WITHOUT CALCULATION,
WITHOUT REASON GOOD OR BAD,
FAITHFULLY, WITH ALL MY HEART
AND SOUL, AND EVERY FACULTY.

Juliette Drouet to Victor Hugo

You have no idea how standoffish I can be with people I don't love. I have brought it to a fine art. But you have broken down my defenses.
And I don't really resent it.

VITA SACKVILLE-WEST TO
VIRGINIA WOOLF

AND I AM FLOATING WITH YOU, IN YOU,
AFLAME AND MELTING—AND A WHOLE LIFE
WITH YOU IS LIKE THE MOVEMENT OF
CLOUDS, THEIR AIRY, QUIET FALLS,
THEIR LIGHTNESS AND SMOOTHNESS,
AND THE HEAVENLY VARIETY OF OUTLINE
AND TINT—MY INEXPLICABLE LOVE.

VLADIMIR NABOKOV TO VÉRA NABOKOV

*My blind eyes
are desperately waiting
for the
sight of you,*

RICHARD BURTON TO
ELIZABETH TAYLOR

NO, NOTHING HAS THE
POWER TO PART
ME FROM YOU; OUR LOVE IS
BASED UPON VIRTUE,
AND WILL LAST AS LONG
AS OUR LIVES.

Voltaire to Catherine Olympe du Noyer

You fear, sometimes,
I do not love you so much
as you wish?
My dear Girl,
I love you ever and ever
and without reserve.

JOHN KEATS TO FANNY BRAWNE

I HURT WITH THE INSATIATE
LONGING, UNTIL I FEEL THAT
THERE WILL NEVER BE ANY RELIEF
UNTIL I TAKE A LONG, DEEP, WILD
DRAUGHT ON YOUR LIPS.

*Warren Harding to
Carrie Fulton Phillips*